MONEY
TO THE POWER OF 10!

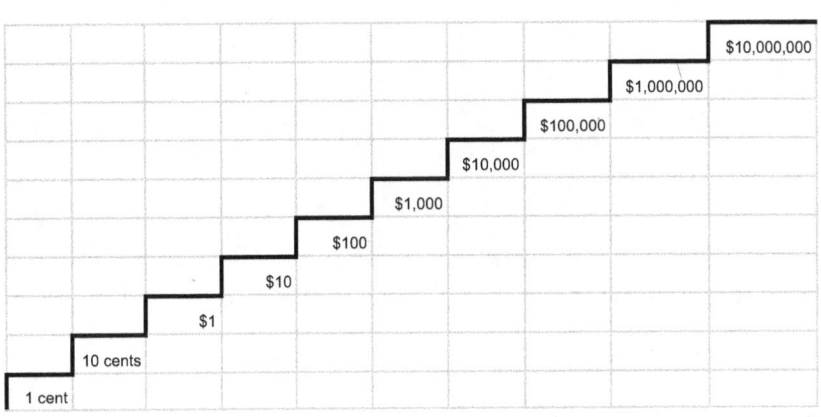

By

Gayland R Jones

Money: To the Power of 10

Copyright © Gayland R Jones 2020

All rights reserved. No part of this publication may be reproduced, distributed, or transmitted in any form whatsoever or by any means (electronic, mechanical, photocopying, recording, or otherwise), or stored in a database or retrieval system without the prior written permission of both the copyright owner and the above publisher, except as permitted under the U.S. Copyright Act of 1976 or for the inclusion quotations in an acknowledged review.

First published in the United States 2020

Printed in the United States of America

Contents

INTRODUCTION	1
INVEST IN YOURSELF	2
ADVICE FOR LIFE	3
MONEY: TO THE POWER OF 10!	4
LEARNING LIVES FOREVER	5
MAINTAIN A CONSTANT FLOW OF INCOME	8
LAW OF FINANCE--TITHING	12
PAY YOURSELF FIRST	14
TELEPHONE	20
ELECTRICITY	22
WATER	24
MORE PAY YOURSELF FIRST TIPS	27
SAVINGS	30
DEBT	33
BUDGET	39
CREDIT CARDS	42
INTEREST	46
NEGOTIATION	49
DISTINGUISH BETWEEN NEEDS AND WANTS	53
INVEST	55
TAXES	61

FLEX$ PLAN (CAFETERIA PLAN) 65
RETIREMENT 69
INSURANCE 74
HOME AND REAL ESTATE 75
MISCELLANEOUS 77
THE 5-FINGER SYSTEM TO FINANCIAL FREEDOM 80
REAL ESTATE INVESTING 83
RETIREMENT 85
MULTIPLE STREAMS OF INCOME 87
3 TIPS TO BECOMING WEALTHY 88
CONCLUSION 90
ABOUT THE AUTHOR 94

Introduction

Sometimes, with all of the double-digit losses on Wall Street, the corporate scandals, government politics, and the fraud, waste, and abuse that are rampant in our society, people don't know what to invest in. They just don't know who to trust, what to do, or where to put their money. This book will help you turn back to the basics and realize in clear and concise steps that you don't necessarily need to depend on other people. You can implement some simple measures to take control of your life. Be steady and consistent. Sometimes less is best. The examples and stories described here will help sprout ideas where you can make more money, spend less, save more, and enjoy your life to the fullest. If you are willing to offer the time, effort, and sacrifice required to become wealthy, this book will help you meet that goal. You can be your best self. You can do it. You can truly invest in yourself.

Invest in Yourself

Investing in yourself is the greatest and most important investment you will ever make. There is no financial investment that will ever match it. Develop yourself, learn skills, and increase your ability and capacity. Let your learning lead to doing and becoming. These are the attributes that will help you obtain a great job, earn more money, and be financially free and happy.

Tony Robbins has said that if you want an average, successful life, it doesn't take much planning. Just stay out of trouble, go to school, and apply for jobs you might like. But, if you want something extraordinary, you have two paths: 1) Become the best at one specific thing. 2) Become very good (in the top 25%) at two or more things.

The first strategy is difficult to nearly impossible. Almost all of us are not professional athletes, star actors, singers, or CEO's of large corporations. So, I would recommend to focus on number two.

The second strategy is easier to accomplish. Everyone has at least a few areas in which they could be in the top 25% with some effort. It's the combination of being good in two areas that will make you stand out and be successful.

Advice for Life

Advice is one thing that is freely given away, but watch that you take only what is worth having. --The Richest Man in Babylon.

Happy are those who dream dreams and are ready to pay the price to make them come true. --L.J. Cardinal Suenens

A penny saved is a penny earned. --Benjamin Franklin

Go confidently in the direction of your dreams. Live the life you've imagined. --Henry David Thoreau

Don't just dream it, be it. --Gayland R Jones

Money: to the Power of 10!

In the graphic on the front cover, there are 10 steps to get from 1 cent to $10,000,000. To take the next step and go from one step to the next, it requires a plan, discipline, and work. With each step, your money grows and increases 10-fold. Each step is 10 times more than the previous step. You can do it. You can achieve great things. As you follow the principles in this book, you can grow your Money: to the Power of 10!

Learning Lives Forever

Successful people are committed to a lifetime of learning. They invest time, energy, and money in improving themselves. Dedicate a little time each day and a few hours each week to actively learning. You can always learn on the job through your experiences, but in addition to that, set aside some time each week to focus solely on learning new skills and developing yourself. This is a great way to invest in yourself. Maximize your potential. Invest in yourself to become great at something. Investing in yourself is the best investment you can make.

There are many ways to learn. Different people have different ways of doing it. Do what works best for you. The way you learn varies depending on what serves you the best. What types of learning do successful people use? Well, here are a few ideas of the more common techniques:

Reading

For many people, reading is fun and they do it for pleasure. They are avid readers. But, just reading for fun is not what I'm talking about here. When you read, read with the purpose to learn new skills. Reading is the preferred way to learn for many successful people.

Experimenting

Quite a few people learn by doing. They are visual learners and need to see it, experiment with it, and do it hands on. Benjamin Franklin and Thomas Edison were like this. They would spend hours methodically doing experiments and testing new theories and ideas. As they experimented, they learned new skills, invented practical products, and solved problems.

Take Classes

A great way to learn new skills and invest in yourself is to take a class, go to a seminar, or go to a conference. You go there to learn that subject matter, and the teacher is there to teach it to you.

Listen to Podcasts

Podcasts can be a good source of information on a particular topic. You can watch them and/or listen to the feed over the internet. There are podcasts out there on a plethora of subjects.

Talk to Experts in the Field

Who better to talk to about learning a new skill in a particular field or area than an expert in that field? Reach out to them and ask them questions about their experiences. Talk to them and have them help you, teach you, and mentor you. You can job-shadow them and get first-hand knowledge of who they are and what they do to be successful.

In today's society and economy, learning new skills is essential to survive the fluid job market, and to thrive. You need to spend time learning so that you will gain the skills you need to elevate your career.

Some people think they don't have time to learn. Well, you can't afford to not take the time to learn. You can either avoid learning and just hope that things go well and that your career continues to advance at its current pace. Or you can invest in yourself and spend time learning new skills so your career will take off and go vertical.

There are many ways to learn, but the point is that you do it. Continually try to learn and want to learn so that you invest in yourself. Learning does live forever.

Maintain a Constant Flow of Income

You have to have money to make money. It takes money to make money.

Have a steady stream of income always coming in. Profitable employment.

One becomes wealthy by establishing a constant flow of income. It is like an everlasting spring. I've seen many mountain streams that never seem to end. They are always providing a continual stream of water. We need to be like springs and maintain a constant flow of income.

Savings are a fine thing, but those who have gotten wealthy didn't get there by saving alone. Savings and investments only preserve what you've gained by other means, by working and following the money.

Get your mind focused on income. This is the first step. Focus on trying to make more money by negotiating a pay increase, searching for a higher paying job, taking on a second job, having your spouse work to contribute to a savings account, and redesigning your budget so you can keep more of your earnings (cut spending). When you increase your income enough, you will be able to save money and follow all the other financial principles discussed herein.

Work

When we do more than we are paid to do, eventually we will be paid more for what we do--Zig Ziglar's Little Instruction Book, page 6.

Work is the foundation of all business, the source of all prosperity, and the parent of genius. It is represented in the humblest savings and has laid the foundation of every fortune.--Anonymous and Zig Ziglar's Little Instruction Book, page 65.

> **Industry is the soul of business and the keystone of prosperity--Charles Dickens.**

Industry. Work is the means whereby dreams become reality. It is work that spells the difference in a person's life. Nothing of real substance comes without work.

Benjamin Franklin in his *Autobiography* said: "Remember that Time is Money....Remember that Credit is Money....Remember that Money is of a prolific generating Nature....In short, the Way to Wealth, if you desire it, is as plain as the Way to Market. It depends chiefly on two words, Industry and Frugality; i.e., Waste neither Time nor Money, but make the best Use of both. He that gets all he can honestly, and saves all he gets (necessary Expenses excepted) will certainly become Rich; If that Being who governs the World, to whom all should look for a Blessing on their Honest Endeavours, doth not in his wise Providence otherwise determine."

Hard work means prosperity, only a fool idles away his time.--Zig Ziglar's Little Instruction Book, page 32.

The Law of the Harvest--whatsoever a man soweth, that shall he also reap--work.

As Henry Wadsworth Longfellow observed:

> The heights by great men reached and kept
> We're not attained by sudden flight,
> But they, while their companions slept,
> We're toiling upward in the night.

An insight that is worth mentioning here is the longer you are able to work, the more money you will make. Thus, for example, if an individual works from the age of 22 (supposing that they completed high school and college) until the age of 70, making an average of $50,000 a year, this individual would have earned $2,400,000 over the course of their 48 working years.

However, if an individual only works from the age of 25 (supposing that they completed high school and college, but only after they took time off to play and they could not decide on a career; thus, they took a few extra years to finish school) until retirement age of 65, making the same average of $50,000 a year, this individual would have earned $2,000,000 over the course of their 40 working years ($400,000 less than the first individual).

Suppose the same factors as the second individual above, but a third individual only works until the age of 55 or 50 because they retire early or have some health problems that will not allow them to continue working. Now this individual would have respectively earned only $1,500,000 over 30 years ($900,000 less than the first individual) or $1,250,000 over 25 years ($1,150,000 less than the first individual).

The moral to this little story is to exercise, eat right, get a good night's sleep, keep yourself healthy, and plan your career and future so you can have the option to work as long as you want. Nevertheless, keep in mind that you want to enjoy life and be successful, but don't burn yourself out and work like a beaten dog. And when it's time to quit, quit, because you do want to enjoy your retirement years. You want to have the option to retire early, or at a reasonable age.

The profile of a wealthy person is this: hard work, perseverance, and most of all, self-discipline. The average wealthy person has lived all his adult life in the same town. He's been married once and is still married. He lives in a middle-class neighborhood next to people with a fraction of his wealth. He's a compulsive saver and investor, and he's made his money on his own. Eighty percent of America's millionaires are first-generation rich. (Doesn't sound like opportunity is dead to me.)--Zig Ziglar's Little Instruction Book, page 25.

Law of Finance-- Tithing

I am a religious person; a Christian. The Lord needs his share. After all, everything we have comes from Him. He expects us to show Him our love by giving back a little of what He has already given us.

The Lord's Law of Finance is Tithing. Regularly pay your tithing each month. Your tithing is one-tenth of your earnings (10%). You can live better off of nine-tenths than you can live off of ten-tenths. The Lord blesses you.

The Lord gave a commandment to ancient Israel through the prophet Malachi: "Bring ye all the tithes into the storehouse,...and prove me now herewith, saith the Lord of hosts, if I will not open you the windows of heaven, and pour you out a blessing, that there shall not be room enough to receive it" (Malachi 3:10).

Some of you have money problems. I know that. There is never enough money in your homes. I know that. You are struggling to get along. What is the cure? The only thing I know of is the payment of tithing. Now, that doesn't mean that you will have a Cadillac and a mansion. But it was God who made the promise that He would open the windows of heaven and pour down blessings upon those who walked honestly with Him in the payment of their tithes and offerings, and He has the capacity to keep His promise. It is my testimony that He does keep that promise. --Gordon B. Hinckley

Yes, I am a God-fearing person. The scriptures say, "But seek ye first the kingdom of God and His righteousness, and all these things shall be added unto you." (Matthew 6:33, 3 Nephi 13:33) What are "these things?" They are food, clothes, a roof over your head, and the necessities of life.

"But before ye seek for riches, seek ye for the kingdom of God. And after ye have obtained a hope in Christ ye shall obtain riches, if ye seek them; and ye will seek them for the intent to do good-- to clothe the naked, and to feed the hungry, and to liberate the captive, and administer relief to the sick and the afflicted." (Jacob 2:18-19)

Pay Yourself First

Pay yourself first. Invest in Yourself.

Establish a rainy-day fund to cover unexpected financial storms.

A portion of what I earn is mine to keep.

In this section, I would like to share the details of some of our purchasing successes, how we gathered our information, and how we have been our own advocates for getting good deals.

Go on work-related, reimbursable business trips:

You don't have to buy food for home, or gas for your vehicle, while you are gone.

You get great per-diem amounts.

You can eat out and live a little.

You get reimbursed for hotel and food.

You get extra money back from your credit card company by charging on your card. Credit card companies will usually pay you between 1% to 5% on your purchases. You can also get credit for airline flights and hotel stays.

You can make extra money because you don't use all of your per-diem amounts.

You save!

I live by this one philosophy: To leave everything better than how I found it.

Don't think that a higher price always means higher quality.

Buy things that are on sale or at a discount, with coupons and deals, like clothes and groceries.

I usually watch gas prices carefully to either make sure that I have a full tank of gas right before prices are going to increase, or to wait and fill up as prices come down. To illustrate my point, the other day I noticed gasoline prices at three different gas stations. The prices were all at the same time, and the gas stations were all within a couple of blocks of each other. The prices were $2.94, $2.99, & $3.06 a gallon, respectively, for regular unleaded gasoline.

Suppose you buy gas once every two weeks for a vehicle that has a fifteen-gallon gas tank. We will use fifteen gallons just for round numbers. The gasoline would cost you $1,146.60, $1,166.10, & $1,193.40 a year, respectively (the price of gas per gallon at each gas station X the fifteen-gallon tank X 26 weeks). Why not buy gas at the cheapest place and respectively save yourself $19.50 and $46.80 a year over the other two gas stations, especially if the cheapest place is only a few blocks away from the more expensive stations?

Now, suppose you buy gas once every week. The gasoline would cost you $2,293.20, $2,332.20, & $2,386.80 a year, respectively (the price of gas per gallon at each gas station X the fifteen-gallon tank X 52 weeks). Why not still buy gas at the cheapest place and respectively save yourself $39.00 and $93.60 a year over the other two gas stations?

Humorous sign by Wilkie Manufacturing of Oklahoma City, Oklahoma was an award winner at the Illinois Sign Association 2005 sign competition. (Photo courtesy ISA)

Gas prices will fluctuate up and down; nevertheless, we can assume that a particular gas station will probably maintain the same cost interval between itself and all the other gas stations. In addition, you may think that one gas station may have better gasoline than another station; however, this thought is not necessarily correct. Based on my own observations, experience, and doing some work for a couple of oil refineries and gas companies, all respected companies' gasolines are relatively the same. Therefore, don't think that you have to patronize one gas station because they have better gasoline than anyone else. You are probably just spending more money for the same quality gas. Also, regular unleaded gasoline is sufficient for most cars and trucks. You don't need to spend extra money on the plus/midgrade or premium octane ratings. Finally, how much money you save, and how much money you spend, will depend on the size of your gas tank and your gasoline usage. You may even have two or three vehicles, so these examples would have to be multiplied two or three times. Your individual circumstances may vary, but the above examples give you an idea of how to invest in yourself by saving money through lower gas prices. I, for one, know that I can spend the $20 to $90 savings on other things besides gasoline for my car.

There are some tips on pumping gas. Only buy or fill up your car or truck in the early morning when the ground temperature is still cold. All service stations have their storage tanks buried below ground. The colder the ground, the more dense the gasoline. When it gets warmer during the day, the gasoline expands. You get more gasoline earlier in the morning.

When you're filling up your tank, don't squeeze the nozzle trigger to fast mode. Pump your gas on a lower mode, thereby minimizing the vapors that are created and losing gas. You don't want your liquid gas to turn to vapor.

A great tip is to fill up when your gas tank is half full. The reason is the more gas you have in your tank the less air is occupying the empty space in the rest of your tank. This slows the evaporation of your gas.

Finally, if there is a gas truck there pumping gas into the storage tanks when you stop to buy gas, do not fill up. The gasoline is most likely being stirred up as the truck is delivering gas. You might pick up some of the dirt in your gas and tank that would normally settle to the bottom with a little time.

By shopping around and getting a good deal, and doing some of our own work, we saved $575 ($1,875 compared to $2,450) on a new roof.

We framed our own basement, painted, did some of the electrical and plumbing work, and did our own landscape and yardwork. Therefore, we saved a lot of money. It helps to be a handyman, knowledgeable in many areas, and learn how to do things.

We bought our couch for $419, because it had a small tear in the back that was easily fixed by the company, instead of for $499. A similar couch at another store cost $799. Therefore, shop around and look for the best deal. We did, and we saved $80 and $380, respectively.

At a point in our life, we wanted to buy a truck. Normally, we would purchase a good, used vehicle because they are only three to five years old, are in good condition, and cost less because depreciation has taken off the brand new effect.

We did some research by talking to a few people, looking online, and looking at a few trucks at some dealerships.

At one dealership, we told a salesman the type of truck we were looking for. He said, "Well then, I have a truck for you." There was a beautiful graphite-colored truck that he had and showed to us. It was basically brand new with only 13 miles on it. An employee had purchased this truck out of two trucks that he was looking at. After he bought it and drove it a couple of miles, he decided he wanted the other truck. This truck then had to technically be sold as used rather than brand new.

So, here we come along and buy an awesome, brand new truck for $12,000 less than what it should have cost. It was a great deal, a great truck, and we were truly blessed!

Just before we had our third child, we decided to get a bunk bed for the other two children. They enjoyed playing together and wanted to be in the same room. Therefore, we went out and looked at some bunk beds. We did some shopping around at about four or five stores, looked at a few ads, and talked to some people we knew. It really didn't take that long to find what we wanted. At one particular store, we found an excellent, sturdy bunk bed for $200. This was the best bunk bed for the price that we had seen. We made the purchase. The clerk told us they would deliver it for free; however, if we wanted them to put it together, it would cost an additional $25. I assured them that I could put it together myself.

The next day, upon their going to locate the bunk bed and deliver it to our house, they discovered that they did not have any more of those bunk beds in stock at that particular time. They asked us if we wouldn't mind taking the showroom bunk bed. You see, we weren't going to have our baby for another month and a half, so we could call the shots on our predetermined timeline. As we had inspected the showroom bunk bed, and knew it to be in excellent condition and of good quality, we asked them if they would deduct $25 for it; otherwise, we were fine with waiting until their next shipment of beds came in. They said that they would deliver this bed to us and deduct the $25. Therefore, in the end, we purchased a great bunk bed, got free delivery, received a $25 savings, and had it assembled for free (it didn't cost me $25 for them to assemble it or take me the time to assemble it myself). By the way, we saved $40 on the mattresses. In total, we saved $90, plus our time, on the deal. In addition, bunk beds and mattresses at other stores around the area would have cost at least $150 to $200 more.

Be frugal.

Thrift. "Thrifty" is one of the twelve points in the Boy Scout Law. I am an Eagle Scout.

Every improvement that we make adds to our wealth.

Make deals and trades.

Fix, wash, and maintain your own car. You can save about $10 to $20 each time by changing your own oil. That adds up to $30 to $60 a year if you change your oil every 3,000 miles and you drive about 10,000 miles a year. You can save money by doing your own, small maintenance jobs. If you change your brakes, you can save about $70 to $100 each time. If you replace your own alternator, you can save about $50 to $100. You save money if you can replace your own hoses and belts, which are fairly easy to replace. And on, and on, and on.

Control your uses of the phone, gas, water, and electricity (utilities), etc. and save money.

Telephone

We as consumers need to control our telephone charges. You do not have to open a phone bill to know that talk really isn't cheap. With the slew of charges that appear on today's telephone statements--from federal taxes and fees to state and local taxes and fees--it is tough to figure out just where your money is going.

Some fees, like line fees, federal taxes and fees, state taxes and fees, local taxes and fees, portability charge fees, and universal service fund fees are pretty much allowable and standard monthly telephone fees. The only ways to reduce these fees are to not use your phone as much (local and long-distance calls), evaluate your plan to see if a change is needed based upon your current calling habits, and shop around and check the competition for better deals.

The first step to saving is to call your telephone service provider and enroll in a discount plan. When you do this, be sure that you check with all of the local and national telephone companies. Shop around and acquire the best plan for you. Do not just settle for the company's basic rates, which are usually the highest, obtain a plan that fits your needs and calling habits.

Basic local service fees is an area that you can adjust if you do not make many local calls. Ask your carrier if you can pay for these calls individually rather than forking over the flat fee for an unlimited or multi-hour plan.

Many companies give you the option of having their basic wire maintenance service. The fee for this service is a few dollars a month, and the fee is like insurance in that it covers you in case the wires or jacks in your home need repair. Since these problems are rare, you could probably drop this service.

Long-distance fees is another area that you can adjust if you do not make many long-distance calls. If you rarely make out-of-town calls, like five or fewer calls a month, you can avoid service fees by dropping your long-distance service. Instead, try those "10-10" dial-around numbers or prepaid phone cards. Some companies offer cards with rates as low as 4 cents a minute.

One good tip to remember is to keep your eyes and ears open for any special telephone plans and deals. If a competing carrier has a better plan, ask your carrier to match it. If they will not match it, then switch immediately. Telephone companies have often tried desperately to acquire people's business. A few years ago, I remember getting a few phone calls a day from various local and national telephone companies. These companies were trying to get us to switch to their service. I remember changing our service three times in about a four-month period to obtain the best phone plans and deals. We made $175 off those companies, and we got one of them to give us 500 extra, free minutes.

Another good tip is to read your telephone bill and watch for monthly minimum fees that you did not expect. Also, watch for "cramming", which is when you are billed for services that you did not order.

Electricity

An energy-savings tip is when buying new appliances, compare energy-efficiency ratings and annual operating costs. A slightly higher initial cost for a high-efficiency appliance could be paid back quickly through energy savings and lower utility bills.

Which appliances do you think have the biggest impact on your energy bill? Here is a list of appliances from most expensive to least expensive: Electric water heater, central air conditioning, refrigerator, incandescent lighting, electric range and oven, clothes dryer, TV, fluorescent lighting, dishwasher, clothes washer, and home computer and printer. By the way, hair dryers are right up there in expensive energy users.

Switch some of your heavy appliance use away from peak hours and towards non-peak hours. Avoid using your dishwasher and washer/dryer during summer peak hours of 2 p.m. to 8 p.m. Run only full loads in the late evenings or on weekends. Open windows to bring in cool air during the morning and evening, then close windows and blinds to keep that cooler air in during the heat of the day. Use portable fans where and when you need them as they use much less electricity than large air-conditioning systems. Set your various thermostats at a consistent temperature, and avoid constantly increasing or decreasing the thermostat temperature. Wash clothes in cold water. Cut back as much as possible on lighting. Switch to compact fluorescent bulbs or LED bulbs in lights that remain on for extended periods of time. These bulbs use about 75% less energy and last about 10 times longer. Also, replace higher watt bulbs with lower watt bulbs in your remaining fixtures. Turn off any lights, appliances, computers, monitors, etc. at night and whenever they are not in use. If you don't mind it and you are able to do it, dry clothes on a clothesline instead of in a dryer. Plant deciduous trees to shade your walls, windows, and roof in the summer to keep your home cooler.

Water

Short-Term

1. Fix leaks inside and outside of your home.

2. Tune up your sprinkler system by replacing broken heads and making sure your sprinkler system works properly. An efficient sprinkler system applies an even distribution of water across your turf area. Make sure sprinklers are not spraying onto roads or other hard surfaces.

3. Do not turn automatic sprinkler clocks on too early in the year. Operate sprinkler systems manually in the spring only when lawn and landscape show signs of needing water. This procedure will encourage roots to grow deeper.

4. Running sprinklers for shorter, multiple runs is better than one long run to minimize water run-off. Many soils cannot absorb water as fast as a sprinkler system can distribute it. For example, rather than running sprinklers for 30 minutes, run them three times for 8-10 minutes.

5. Do not water from 10:00 a.m. to 6:00 p.m. to cut down on evaporation losses during the heat of the day.

6. Schedule a "water check" with trained professionals from the water company to evaluate your water needs.

Long-Term

1. If you are landscaping for the first time, consider water conserving plants and turf grasses. Existing yards may also be retrofitted with water conserving plants. Also, a well-designed sprinkler system may cost a little more up-front, but will save water and dollars in the long-run.

2. Consider zonal designs for your sprinkler system that apply water at different rates according to the water requirements of the areas you are watering. For example, trees and shrubs may have different watering requirements than turf grasses.

3. Use landscaping fabrics and mulches to minimize evaporation losses.

By paying these above-mentioned utility bills of telephone, electricity, water, and similar type bills automatically and online, you can wait until close to the deadline before paying them, the payment will go through almost instantaneously at that time, there won't be a chance of the payment getting lost in the mail, and you won't have the cost of buying checks, stamps, and envelopes.

MORE PAY YOURSELF FIRST TIPS

Control your vices of smoking, drinking, gambling, and lottery expenses. By cutting down their uses, or by not doing them at all, you save a lot of money. I can say I have never smoked, drank, or so much as put even one penny into a slot machine. The odds and machines are stacked against you. The chances of winning big are almost zero. You can look up PBS.org's Frontline: The Odds of Gambling to see how the odds are against you.

Do not get swept up by the promises of "easy money", "get rich quick", and other cliches that hint at financial freedom. If something seems too easy and you do not have to put forth any effort to achieve it, it is probably too good to be true.

There are many of these "easy money" schemes out there that are on the rise. One of these money schemes, which you hear a lot about and you seem to see ads for everywhere, is the work-at-home stuffing envelopes scheme. This scheme starts with many marketing tools and unfounded guarantees. Then, the perpetrators persuade you to send $50, $100, $300, and even $500 to order their kit and get moving towards your financial goals. Once you send your advance payment, you never hear back from them. You should never send anyone an advance payment unless you have done your homework and research to ensure that the entity and program are legitimate.

Work-at-home schemes typically require money up front in exchange for information and materials to do a job. The jobs are often medical billing for physicians, stuffing envelopes, and making crafts.

The Better Business Bureau recorded 5,561 complaints nationwide about work-at-home schemes. This number is a 40% increase over the 3,967 complaints logged two years prior. The bureau also received nearly 280,000 inquiries from consumers about potential work-at-home programs, making it the most asked-about business. A nationwide study of 112 programs by the bureau found that only two programs might have been legitimate.

Therefore, just be happy with who you are and what you have. Don't always think that there are greener pastures somewhere else. Sure, it is fine to want to improve, progress, and become financially free; however, do not go looking all over the world for something that is in your own backyard and right under your nose. Deal with the things that you can do and the things that you can control.

Sell your junk (yard sales) or just flat out don't buy junk, knick-knacks, and things you can't use.

Save money by obeying city, county, state, and federal laws, etc. Don't pay fines and forfeitures. Not wearing a seat belt will cost you $45. It will cost you various, other amounts for speeding, improper lane change (signal), and car not in working condition.

While working as a Senior Auditor for the Utah State Auditor's Office, I audited various District, Juvenile, and Justice Courts. According to the Uniform Fine & Bail Schedule, it would cost you $120 if you received a ticket for going 0-10 miles an hour over the speed limit. There are many other felonies and misdemeanors that would cost a lot more.

I have my wife cut my hair. She does a good job of it. If you're like me and have a fast-growing, thick head of hair, you have to get your hair cut once a month. By having my wife cut my hair, I save from $10 - $15 a month and $120 to $180 a year.

One year, we asked the city and county if they had any planned clean-up or beautification days. They said that they did during a certain week of April. Then we asked them if they had any free vouchers for residents to take their garbage to the landfill during that week. They said that they did. Therefore, we waited until the appropriate time, pruned our trees, did some landscaping, and performed the routine spring-cleaning items. Then we hauled off a load to the landfill. From our diligent planning, we saved the $25 fee of hauling a load of trash to the dump.

Win-win situations.

Make contracts, and build networks, politics, you scratch my back, I'll scratch yours.

Collect early, pay later but not late.

Live within your means.

Live on less than you make.

Savings

Pay yourself a little money each month, like 10%, via a savings account so that you have cash on hand for financial emergencies and desired purchases. A savings account can offer great peace of mind because it provides a buffer between spending and debt.

When I was a young boy, I had a piggy bank. My parents encouraged me to save part of everything I earned. I felt good when my piggy bank was full. When I got a little older, my mother took me to the local bank to open a savings account. Some financial institutions offer what they call a "Money Bunny" savings program for young kids to help them get started on a successful savings program. As these children grow into teenagers, these same financial institutions have what they call a "Personal Stash" account.

It's a good feeling to have a couple month's salary put away in a savings account.

If you wish to get rich, save what you get. A fool can earn money, but it takes a wise man to save and dispose of it to his own advantage. --Brigham Young

There are a variety of options available to assist you with your savings' needs. For example: Regular savings accounts, money-market accounts, certificates of deposit, individual retirement accounts, and more.

A new car, college, marriage, and other known future expenses necessitate saving and financial planning. Good short-term and long-term savings plans can greatly reduce the financial burden associated with near-future events and more distant future events, depending on the time-frame of these expenses.

It is the end of the month and there is not enough money to buy all of the things we seem to need, let alone the things we want. As we struggle to make ends meet, we think about the need for a savings program, but it seems there is just not enough money to begin one. If we weigh the cost of waiting to start a savings plan, however, we might be more motivated to find the funds and begin. Let's look at the benefits of maintaining both short-term savings and long-term investments. The actual dollar amounts noted are only for the purpose of illustrating the concepts.

Short-term savings: These savings are used for emergencies, buying or repairing vehicles, or replacing household furnishings and appliances. The cost to the consumer who doesn't save regularly for such expenses can be enormous, as the following example illustrates.

The Robinsons bought a car for $15,000, with a $500 down payment. They financed the balance, $14,500, for five years at an interest rate of 9.5 percent, requiring a monthly payment of $377.46. At the end of five years, they had paid out $19,834.16 on the loan.

The Clarks, however, did not have a down payment. They decided to drive their old car five more years and put $250 in the bank every month earning 6 percent interest. At the end of five years, they had deposited $15,000. But the Clarks' money had also been earning interest, giving them a total of $18,762.28 in the bank. After paying cash for their car, they still had $3,762.28 in their savings account. Even after subtracting the cost of car repairs on their older vehicle, the Clarks had money left to invest.

Long-term savings: College costs and retirement funds are the main reasons people begin a long-term savings program. The key to making successful long-term investments is to start as early as possible.

Let's say we have two young couples. The husbands are both 23 years old. Each couple decides to budget $1,000 a year for savings and investments. Couple number one opens an Individual

Retirement Account (IRA), tax-deferred, at 8 percent interest annually, and puts $1,000 a year into it each year for the next 10 years. Then their circumstances change, and they can no longer make deposits to their IRA.

Couple number two, on the other hand, decides to spend their money in the early years of their marriage on home furnishings and other things they feel the need to get started. Ten years later they decide to open an IRA account and deposit $1,000 per year at 8 percent interest, which they continue to do faithfully each year for the next 32 years, until they retire.

What is the result of each couple's investment when they reach age 65? Couple number one has $217,937.49 in their IRA, of which only $10,000 was their own money. Couple number two, however, had accumulated only $184,273.61 in their IRA, but had invested $32,000 of their own money. They could have acquired much more money had they begun their savings plan earlier than they did.

The cost of putting off the start of a regular savings program is one few of us can afford.

Debt

> Debt is the worst poverty--Thomas Fuller.

Thomas Jefferson said, "Never spend your money before you have it", and "Never buy what you do not want, because it is cheap; it will be dear to you."

Debt is a ticking bomb. First, you don't plan, you don't balance your budget, and you don't save. Then, you cannot control your spending habits so your bills start piling up. Next, you become delinquent (30 days past due) on your credit cards, mortgages, and other consumer debt. Finally, when utilities skyrocket, you become unemployed, or another event occurs, the debt-bomb explodes. You become bankrupt and are in a state of financial shambles and ruin.

There are certain occasions beyond one's control that can send you into debt, besides mere foolish money decisions, like a terminal illness, an accident, crime, or money fraud. While it's our foolish decisions that often lead us into debt, other factors may play into it as well.

Many people buy things just because they have a coupon for it, or because it's a good deal. However, they probably don't need it, or even really want it. So why not save that money by not making the purchase, or spend that money on something you really need.

Pay your bills when they are due, but not way before. You might as well earn that extra interest yourself than allow another business to get your money early and earn the interest on it. However, do ensure that you pay your bills on time. If your payment is late, you will pay hefty penalties.

People are always trying to "keep up with the Joneses". Now, even though this is my last name, following this cliche isn't necessarily a good thing. When one family in the neighborhood gets a boat, a new car, or other fancy toys, the others think they "need" these things too. "To satisfy our desires, we go into debt, dissipate our resources in the payment of high interest, and become like indentured servants working to pay off our debts."-- Gordon B. Hinckley

Make timely payment of obligations a cardinal principle in your lives.

If you cannot obtain all that you wish for today, then learn to do without the things that you cannot purchase and pay for now.

Maintain a good credit history.

Don't go into debt (credit cards, buying and paying interest) except for a house and maybe a car.

Are you a slave or a free man?

Are you free, or are you a slave to money?

One of the principal causes of the distress that exists in the world today is that people are living beyond their means. They have borrowed largely, mortgaged their homes, and nearly everything they possess, to keep pace with their neighbors, competing with each other in putting on appearances.

Many of us are covetous. We desire in our hearts to have everything our neighbor has whether we need it or not. In order to be like our neighbor; in order that we may associate with him, we must have as fine a house, as costly of furniture, and as many luxuries whether we can afford it as well as our neighbor can or not. Now, all of this is extremely foolish.

If you desire to prosper, and to be free, you must first meet your obligations to God, and then you must meet your obligations to your fellowmen.

Debt can be a terrible thing. It is so easy to incur and so difficult and laborious to repay. Borrowed money is had only at a price, and that price can be burdensome. Bankruptcy generally is the bitter fruit of debt, overextension, and uncontrolled appetites. It is a tragic culmination of a simple process of borrowing more than one can repay.

"He who spends more than he earns is sowing the winds of needless self-indulgence from which he is sure to reap the whirlwinds of trouble and humiliation."--The Richest Man in Babylon.

Don't buy things if we are unable to pay for them.

I recognize that it may be necessary to borrow to get a home, of course. But let us buy a home that we can afford and thus ease the payments which will constantly hang over our heads without mercy or respite for as long as 30 years.

If there is any one thing that will bring peace and contentment into the human heart, and into the family, it is to live within our means. And if there is any one thing that is grinding and discouraging and disheartening, it is to have debts and obligations that one cannot meet--Gordon B. Hinckley.

D&C 104:78-80, 82

And again, verily I say unto you, concerning your debts--behold it is my will that you shall pay all your debts. And it is my will that you shall humble yourselves before me, and obtain this blessing by your diligence and humility and the prayer of faith. And inasmuch as you are diligent and humble, and exercise the prayer of faith, behold, I will soften the hearts of those to whom you are in debt, until I shall send means unto you for your deliverance. And inasmuch as ye are humble and faithful and call upon my name, behold, I will give you the victory.

Experian.com states that consumer debt has increased nearly $2.3 trillion since the height of the Great Recession in 2009--

growing across almost all debt products. Consumer debt has grown 19% since 2009 to its current record high of $14.1 trillion in 2019. The average household debt is over $135,000. According to NerdWallet, over 67 million households in the United States carry credit card balances. These balances average $6,849 and cost $1,162 per year in interest and fees. Student loan debt tops $1.5 trillion, and the average household owes $46,459 in student loans. In 2019, the Federal Reserve measured household debt as a percentage of disposable income at over 15 percent.

Everyone knows that every dollar borrowed carries with it the penalty of paying interest. We are beguiled by seductive advertising. Television carries the enticing invitation to borrow up to 125 percent of the value of one's home. But no mention is made of interest. When money cannot be repaid, then bankruptcy follows. There were 751,186 personal bankruptcies in the United States in 2018, per the American Bankruptcy Institute. The number has been decreasing in recent years because of the Bankruptcy Abuse Prevention and Consumer Protection Act that was passed in 2005.

According to Time Magazine, the #1 reason to file for bankruptcy is loss of job. Although there are other reasons given to file for bankruptcy (46%--medical reasons, 19%--family breakup, 7%--birth of a child, 5%--car accident, and 4%--death in the family), especially unexpected events, most people file just because they lost their job.

Too many people live from paycheck to paycheck. Where do you think the term "payday lending" comes from? People run out of money before their next payday, and the lender may charge up to $40 for a $200 loan to be repaid in two weeks. That's an annual interest rate of 521%. In exchange for the advance, the lender requires the borrower to write a check for $240, dated to coincide with his next paycheck. When the two weeks are up, the borrower may repay the loan or roll it over into a new one, further increasing the interest charges. If the borrower fails to do either, the lender cashes the post-dated check. If it bounces, the lender sues, and in some states, collects up to three times the value of the check, plus interest. It's like getting on a treadmill. Once you get on it, you can't get off. Because these individuals did not put money away in a "rainy-day" fund, they cannot maneuver the little bumps in the road. Even more so, when large bumps come along they are devastated.

In 2019, Americans filed approximately 764,000 consumer-bankruptcy petitions that erased more than $113 billion in debt--that translates into more than $1,130 per household in higher costs for goods, services, and credit. Those losses are passed on to other consumers, resulting in a hidden tax for every American household.

Bankruptcy can make grown men cry. Many people take the financial crises as a sign of personal failure. Despite their treading water through partial payments, the balance on their outstanding debt never goes down. A government study showed that by the time individuals and families seek bankruptcy protection, more than 20% of income before taxes is going toward paying interest and fees on their unsecured debt.

Once a family is over 30% debt-to-income ratio, it should stop using unsecured credit. But people don't know that. They think that just because they've been approved for this higher credit limit, they can manage it. Because many people pay only the minimum amount due or a few dollars more, they think that everything is fine. But the balance on the cards continues to grow, more as a result of the interest than the use of the cards.

Nothing is quite as discouraging and debilitating as debt and obligations that one cannot meet. Self-reliance cannot be obtained when there is serious debt hanging over a household. One has neither independence nor freedom from bondage when obligated by debts. Being free of debt contributes to our financial comfort and, more importantly, to a sense of great personal freedom and peace of mind.

Dr. James Clayton, professor of history and former dean of the graduate school at the University of Utah, has specialized, throughout his distinguished career, in the evaluation of economic history. Dr. Clayton said: "Back in the 1950's, 30 percent of [our] disposable income was debt. Now 92 percent of [our] disposable income is debt. The average American household has spent next year's entire income, and that is unprecedented in our history. Our savings rate is very, very low. A couple of weeks ago, it went below zero. That has not been true since the 1930's.

A note of interest is that not all debt is bad. In fact, sound business debt and reasonable debt for education are elements of growth. Sound mortgage credit is a real help to a family that must borrow for a home. If you must incur debt to meet the reasonable necessities of life, then, as you value your solvency and happiness, buy within your means. Resist the temptation to plunge into a property far more pretentious or spacious than you really need.

Many people do not have the know-how, are not disciplined enough, or do not want to be bothered themselves with paying their bills. Or maybe they are just trying to juggle their bills and avoid bankruptcy. At any rate, more and more individuals are using debt-service companies to help them consolidate their debts and eventually get out of debt. These companies are supposed to deduct money from their clients' accounts and make the debt payments as they become due. However, many of these companies are poorly mismanaged. The companies often go out of business, go bankrupt, and/or get sued--sometimes criminally. The very thing people were trying to avoid actually happens--that their credit becomes marred and they get deeper in debt. If the problem isn't remedied soon, the individuals could lose their homes and everything they have. Many people find out soon that they have to be educated and pay their bills on their own. Therefore, I would submit to you that you should not get involved with any of these debt-service companies. Just budget your expenses, stay on top of your bills, and don't pay these companies' wages. You can handle your bills on your own.

Budget

Budget, plan.

Control your expenses.

Budget your expenses so that you will have money to pay for your necessities, then to pay for your worthwhile enjoyments and wants without spending more than nine-tenths (tithing) of your earnings.

Avoiding the grasp of unnecessary debt requires that we control or, in some cases, change our spending habits. Establish a budget, but keep it flexible enough to avoid frustration, If necessary, seek financial advice. As a family, discuss your financial situation so that each member understands the family's monetary constraints. Review the family's financial progress each month. Good financial planning often enables us to afford things that, if purchased compulsively, could lead to unnecessary debt.

Sticking to a budget allows you to enjoy a higher standard of living. Having a financial plan helps you to see many areas where you might be wasting money and enables you to get more of what you really want.

A budget is like having an empty container, a container filled with big rocks, and a container filled with very small rocks. If you first fill the empty container with all of the little expenses or things that you want (small rocks), then you do not have enough room to fit the large expenses or necessities (large rocks).

However, if you first fill the empty container with the large expenses (large rocks), then you will still have enough room for the small expenses (small rocks).

This way you can stretch your money, make it to the end of the month, and pay all of your bills, often with enough money left over to purchase a few wants. You just have to budget properly, be creative, and go about things the right way.

Images Credit: Institute for Integrative Nutrition

A budget is a plan of how to save and spend money, not just a record of how it is spent. As you set up a budget, one of the challenges might be your differing views on how your income should be spent or saved. Budgeting requires open and honest communication with one another to work out your differences. Each of you will have to stay within the parameters of your budget, otherwise it will be useless. Initially this might seem confining, but once you commit yourselves fully, you will begin to feel some of the freedom budgeting brings, including peace of mind. Budgeting will help you gain control over your money, eliminate impulse buying, and put aside money for future needs.

As part of your budget, you might want to set up two savings accounts: One long-term account and one short-term account.

Your long-term savings account will consist of future reserves. You might want to have a goal to have a six-month supply of money in the bank and to consistently save money for your children's education and weddings.

Your short-term savings account could include such items as insurance, taxes, car maintenance, home improvements, gifts and holidays, and clothing. You might want to budget a specific amount each pay period for each category, allowing the balances to build up over time. Then, when you need money for one of those expenses, it is already there. Another benefit that comes from having the money set aside is that you can buy items when they are on sale without compromising your budget or turning to credit cards.

Your short-term savings account will also enable you to save for large purchases. Saving for these purchases will assist you to buy without going into debt and incurring large interest charges.

Credit Cards

Don't buy credit card insurance for lost or stolen credit cards, because you can always call and cancel the card. Also, the law states that you are only liable for $50, even if the thief maxes out your credit card. Now, a debit card, or bank card, is a different story. You can be liable for whatever amount is in your checkbook.

Experian.com says that Americans, on average, carry four credit cards and have 486 million credit card accounts in 2019. The value charged on their VISA, MasterCard, Discover, and American Express accounts per year is about $4 trillion.

Some credit card companies have programs that supposedly "protect" your credit. If you become involuntarily unemployed, become disabled, or become hospitalized, (with various requirements, stipulations, and restrictions of course) no finance charges will occur and no monthly payments will be required for a certain period of time. First of all, individuals should not get heavily into debt and carry such high balances on their credit cards. Second, what are employer-provided programs and insurance for if they are not there to protect you and help you in these circumstances? Of course for this extra-special, credit protection, the credit card companies charge you a monthly fee. The fee is about 70 cents per $100 of your average daily balance, with a maximum monthly fee of $24.50. This fee can add up quickly and the fee is "conveniently" billed to your account. Some companies offer you free trial periods, and guess what, when the trial period is up, they automatically bill your credit card unless you go through the hassle of calling them or writing them so they will stop the service. I personally do not think it is a good idea to become involved with these programs. These programs are geared to take your hard-earned money away from you and allow these companies to get rich.

Pay with cash whenever possible, and avoid the temptation to use credit cards. A widely accepted credit card is useful in emergencies and in situations when carrying cash may be unwise, such as during a vacation. But credit cards usually carry high interest rates, and their convenience can easily lead to unnecessary debt. If you are tempted to make impulsive purchases because of the convenience of using credit cards, make it a policy to wait 24 hours before acting so you can consider the purchase more objectively.

A credit card trick that I use to invest in myself is outlined below. (Note that using credit cards is not always bad if you are smart, pay off your balance in full, and do not go into debt.)

You use your credit card, and say you spend $1,000 a month, just for round numbers. You receive a bill every month for your charges, and it is due in a few weeks. If you write a check out from your checking account for the entire balance, put it in an envelope, and write the deadline on the envelope, you can mail the bill about a week before the due date and have it be received right on time. With today's technology, you can pay your credit card, and many of your other monthly bills, with automatic payment (auto-pay) on the due date. You can also negotiate the monthly due date to be the same day of the month so you don't have to keep track of so many dates. You can get most of your bills paid at the same time each month, and you can make sure it is after you get paid so you have money in your account to pay your bills. This procedure allows you to pay for most of the items you buy more than a month after you receive them. The best part about this procedure is that you pay zero percent interest on the debt, and you have roughly the $1,000 extra in your account at all times. This extra money can earn more interest if it's in your money market account. Therefore, this little analogy shows that interest-free debt is not a bad thing, as long as you do not live from paycheck to paycheck. The smartest thing about this tactic is that you can start taking money back from the credit card companies.

We think we need a larger home, with a three-car garage, and a recreational vehicle parked next to it. We long for designer clothes, extra TV sets, all with the latest in streaming, the latest model computers, and the newest car. Often these items are purchased with borrowed money, without giving any thought to providing for our future needs. The result of all this instant gratification is overloaded bankruptcy courts and families that are far too preoccupied with their financial burdens.

Live strictly within your income and save something for a rainy day. Incorporate into your lives the discipline of budgeting. As regularly as you pay your tithing, set aside an amount needed for future family requirements.

Avoid excessive debt. Necessary debt should be incurred only after careful, thoughtful consideration and after obtaining the best possible advice. We need the discipline to stay well within our ability to pay. We need to avoid debt as we would avoid the plague.

Live within your means. Get out of debt. Keep out of debt. Lay by for a rainy day which has always come and will come again. Practice and increase your habits of thrift, industry, economy, and frugality.

Incurrence of debt is such an enticement. Accompanying the ease with which we can obtain debt should be the great caution of avoidance. Take the opportunity to compute how much you would add to your personal net worth if your home mortgage was only for ten or fifteen years instead of thirty. Compute the value of sweat equity if your time and your talents are invested in adding to the size and comfort of your home.

It is easy to let consumer debt get out of hand. If you do not have the discipline to control the use of credit cards, it is better not to have them. A well-managed family does not pay interest--it earns it. A good definition for interest is "Thems that understands interest receives it, thems that don't pays it."

Some necessities such as a home and an education may require that we incur long-term debt. But the relative ease with which we may qualify to secure a loan should not be an excuse to live beyond our means. My wife and I were both working and we qualified for a $212,000 home loan. However, we did not get ourselves that far in debt. We bought a $130,000 home instead.

"It is important to learn to distinguish between wants and needs. It takes self-discipline to avoid the 'buy now, pay later' philosophy and to adopt the 'save now and buy later' practice.

Owning a home free of debt is an important goal of provident living. Homes that are free and clear of mortgages and liens cannot be foreclosed on.

Independence means being free of personal debt and of the interest and carrying charges required by debt the world over."

By controlling debt, we have greater peace of mind, financial security, independence, and comfort.

What a wonderful feeling it is to be free of debt, to have a little money against a day of emergency put away where it can be retrieved when necessary. Look to the condition of your finances. Be modest in your expenditures. Discipline yourselves in your purchases to avoid debt to the extent possible. Pay off debt as quickly as you can, and free yourselves from bondage.

Interest

Interest never sleeps nor sickens nor dies. Once in debt, interest is your companion every minute of the day and night; you cannot shun it or slip away from it; you cannot dismiss it; it yields neither to entreaties, demands, or orders; and whenever you get in its way or cross its course or fail to meet its demands, it crushes you.

"To satisfy our desires, we go into debt, dissipate our resources in the payment of high interest, and become as slaves working to pay it off. I commend to you the virtues of thrift and industry. It is work and thrift that make the family independent."

When people borrow money, they pay a fee, or interest, for the privilege of using money that is not their own. In effect, debt allows the current use of future income, but that privilege often carries a heavy penalty in high interest costs.

2 Kings 4:7 in the Bible says, "Pay thy debt, and live." Proverbs 22:7 says, "the borrower is servant to the lender." The Apostle Paul instructed the Romans to "owe no man any thing" (Rom. 13:8). "Reasonable debt for the purchase of an affordable home and perhaps for a few other necessary things is acceptable. But from where I sit, I see in a very vivid way the terrible tragedies of many who have unwisely borrowed for things they really do not need."

It is possible to buy almost anything today without money in hand--at least until the first payment comes due. Many companies work hard to create a mind-set in which consumers *expect* to go into debt to buy their products. Some businesses have even created their own finance companies for that purpose.

Advertising for these products boldly offers "no-hassle financing" or "easy credit terms." Some financial institutions advertise that a debt-financed vacation would relieve stress. The media constantly bombards us with the message *You can have it all today.*

The temptation to plunge into debt may be greater than ever. Banks are competing furiously against one another to lend, and therefore, they are deluging consumers with credit-card offers. Some advertise "no payments until next year." Remember that delayed payments often result in high interest costs and must all eventually be paid in full.

The ease of obtaining credit has become a significant source of temptation to some people, many of whom may eventually find themselves trapped by debt. Sometimes credit-card debt soars to thousands or tens of thousands of dollars for an individual or a family, often with little to show for it. Another problem arises when personal items that are debt-financed, such as cars, drop in value faster than the loan on them is repaid. "Debt can be a terrible thing. It is so easy to incur and so difficult to repay. Borrowed money is had only at a price, and that price can be burdensome."

"Now is the time to pay off obligations....Let us use the opportunity we have to speed up repayment of mortgages and to set aside provisions for education, possible periods of decreased earning power, and emergencies the future may hold"--Gordon B. Hinckley. Interest costs can be reduced dramatically by simply speeding up payments on all outstanding loans.

Sometimes people borrow the maximum amount possible approved on their loan when buying a house because interest costs can be deducted from their personal income taxes. However, keep in mind that the amount saved in taxes represents only a portion of the interest paid out. You do not get a dollar of tax benefit for every dollar of interest paid. Some financial experts suggest that people would be better off with a smaller mortgage and investing the difference.

By paying extra money on the mortgage principal each month, homeowners may realize significant savings. Reducing a home mortgage provides a *guaranteed* return on the amount prepaid. Even a relatively small amount added to the monthly principal payment can produce dramatic returns. For example, payments on a 30-year home mortgage of $100,000 at 9 percent run $804.62 a month. If merely 10 percent, or $80.46, is added to the mortgage payment each month, the mortgage would be paid off 9 years sooner, saving $67,000!

Negotiation

Negotiating is a life strategy. Over time, as you practice negotiating, you can build wealth and create stronger personal and professional relationships. We should always strive to develop our talents and further our skills--negotiating being one of them.

People have different negotiating styles. Some people are quick to act and make decisions. Maybe they know what they want or they are just trying to fluster the other party. Other people are more slow and deliberate. They want the other party to think and wonder about the next move to make. They do not want to give away any secrets.

When we negotiate, we need to remember that everything is negotiable. We can always ask for more or for a better deal--and remember, we can say no if we don't like the deal.

Some experiences that I have had while negotiating have been:

I have bought a couple of new suits and had them throw in a tie and a belt for free.

I have made deals for the best room rate on hotel reservations.

I have purchased airline tickets for a better price by letting the airline(s) know that I have searched the Internet and been shopping around.

I have negotiated with my banker for a higher interest rate on a certificate of deposit. We called all of the banks in the area to find out what their going interest rate was on a CD. We approached our bank with the idea of investing in a CD; however, we wanted them to match the highest interest rate at one of the other banks, or we would just go invest our money there. They agreed to give us the higher interest rate if we would invest our money with them.

When we had our second child, everything worked out just fine with the delivery, the baby, and the payment of the bill. However, two years later, as the insurance company was doing an internal audit, they discovered that they had paid too much on our hospital bill. They decided to retract part of their payment to the hospital. Therefore, the hospital performed their own quality review, and they supposedly discovered that we had received certain services for which we had not paid. That is when the hospital came after us for a measly $141.12. They notified us of their finding.

We could not believe it because the birth occurred two years previous. We thought that everything had been taken care of and was long forgotten. Surely there was a statute of limitations on this sort of thing. Well, we found out that they could review these types of issues for up to three years. We decided to do some research and we reviewed all of our old bills and received services. What we found was that they had never billed us for the services in question. In fact, we had a copy of a form from the insurance company that stated "the provider has accepted this as payment in full." We wrote the hospital a letter to that effect and sent copies of this form, invoices, payments, and what we could find relating to laws dealing with the issue.

The hospital reviewed our information and then was able to provide us a detailed bill of the provided services. After our review of the bill, and because we actually had received those certain services, we decided to pay 1/3 ($47.04) of the outstanding bill. However, we wrote "Paid in Full if Cashed or Deposited" on the check (they did deposit our check), and we discussed the issue with the hospital. We strongly persuaded them that they should be obligated to write off 1/3 of the bill for not fulfilling their duty of promptly notifying us of the provided services and properly invoicing us for the correct amount.

You know, the healthcare industry is so messed up anyway. Doctors and hospitals send you thousands of statements, invoices, etc., with some saying to pay and some saying not to pay that it is a wonder anybody can fully understand what is going on. In fact, there are some companies springing up, which are headed by former claims processors, hospital employees, etc. who are trying to help average people understand the complicated claims process.

Anyway, the hospital admitted that they had not fully done their job and conceded to write off about $50 of the total bill. We felt good about our efforts and we had saved $50 by a little negotiating.

In addition to the hospital, the insurance company also did not fulfill their duty of providing us with an explanation of benefits. They had paid a certain amount, and then incorrectly retracted part of that payment. We printed off some information from their website that enumerated certain policies they had in regards to processing claims, one of the items being that they were supposed to provide an explanation of benefits. We sent that information, along with the information we had sent to the hospital, to the insurance company. It all went to their first level appeals process. They then denied the claim and wrote back to us of their decision.

I know that the insurance companies and the hospitals seem to have standard policies of just denying claims and sending the information back to the individuals right away. They just want to throw the ball back in your court and make you deal with it, even though it is not your problem or fault. Sometimes they won't return your phone calls, and then they send you these letters that state you better pay within a specified amount of time or your case will be sent to collections. They try to put fear into you, by trying to get you to act within say 30 days, even though it was their fault for two years.

Well, I wasn't going to be buffaloed by these tactics because I knew that we had ground to stand on. These were unfair claims practices. Therefore, we sent another letter, along with a lot of the same information, back to the insurance company to their second level appeals process. After about 30 days, they had their panel of individuals review the claim, the information, the insurance contract, etc. They wrote back to us basically saying that they were sorry for the inconvenience and thanking us for bringing this matter to their attention. Instead of their paying 1/3 of the claim, as we were asking, they conceded to pay the full amount of the almost $150. They paid the money to the hospital, the hospital paid us back the amount we had paid them, and the whole process was finalized.

If we had just given in to the hospital's and insurance company's tactics, by getting scared and just paying the bill in full with no questions asked, we would have paid $150 bucks for nothing. You have to ask the questions, find out the information, and stick to what you know is true and right. By writing a few letters and taking a little time to correct the problem, we felt a sense of accomplishment and saved ourselves $150.

We got four free oil changes just for listening to the mechanic and coming in on a slower day during a slower time.

What you achieve in life is in direct proportion to how well you negotiate.

Distinguish Between Needs and Wants

Beware of little expenses; a small leak will sink a great ship-- Benjamin Franklin.

People sacrifice tomorrow for what they want today.

If you're not enough without it, you'll never be enough with it.

Prioritize. Control your expenditures. Just because you have a coupon for something, doesn't necessarily mean that you have to have it, and should buy it. Instead of saving 50 cents on a $10.00 item that you don't need, why not save the $10.00 by simply not purchasing the item. Use coupons for items that you would already normally purchase - things you use regularly. There may be the rare exception when you will use a coupon because it brings the cost of something you want to buy down to a price that is reasonable to you. But, as a rule, only use coupons for items you already buy.

All of us seem to have more desires than we can satisfy. First, we need to budget our expenses so we can pay for our needs, then we can pay for our worthwhile wants with the extra.

Ours is a wasteful generation. Our pioneer forebears lived by the motto: "Fix it up, wear it out, make it do, or do without." I have also had to live by that motto various times. You would be amazed at what duct tape and bailing wire can fix. Today, the obsession with riches cankers and destroys and leads to irresponsible financial decisions.

Growing up in a small town and working on the farm helped me out a lot. We didn't have a lot of money or material resources, so we had to work hard and make do with what we had.

We would do well to look to the condition of our personal finances, to be modest and prudent in our expenditures, to discipline our purchasing and avoid debt to the extent possible, to pay off debt quickly, and to free ourselves from the bondage of others.

Wants and needs relate to our society's constant focus on everything we don't have instead of focusing and feeling peace and contentment with all the things we do have. All you have to do to feel content in our society is to look at some of the lesser-developed countries where people struggle daily just to obtain the necessities of life - food, clothing, and shelter. Consider the many comforts of life we enjoy. It is a great idea in many instances to be content with what we already have in life.

Invest

Put money away (savings, CD, mutual funds (diversify). Invest prudently and wisely. Do it while you're young. Time is on your side. Opportunity waits for no man. Today it is here; soon it is gone. Therefore, delay not!

Time: Your Best Investment

If you wonder what you gain or lose by waiting for the right time to invest, perhaps this small illustration will help. We'll assume you want to retire at age 65. At an 8% return, a dollar compounded monthly...

- --at age 25 will increase in value 23.3 times
- --at age 35 will increase in value 9.9 times
- --at age 45 will increase in value 3.9 times
- --at age 55 will increase in value 1.2 times

This is amazing, isn't it? And this is just for a balance that isn't added to. Imagine what regular contributions to the investment will produce! The earlier you start investing, the better off you will be. Utah Retirement System's *ViewPoint*, Volume 18, Number 1.

We now witness an almost cyclical pattern of wide and fearsome swings in the markets of the world. The economy is a fragile thing. A stumble in the economy in England or Japan can immediately affect not only investors but private citizens throughout the world.

Multiply your investment. Don't invest in purposes with which you are not familiar.

Checking, balance it (money) with your statements.

Giving loans are investments. However, you do not want to risk losing your money that you labored so much to acquire. Therefore, lend it to those individuals that you feel confidently will promptly pay it back.

Compound interest, annuities, systematic investment plan.

Take advantage of all of your opportunities. If you don't, they will be gone. The windows don't stay open forever. Start when you're young. The earlier you start, the wealthier you will become.

The rule of 72 on interest:

By learning one simple rule you can become a whiz at calculating the performance of your investments. It's called the rule of 72, and it works like this.

If you want to know how long it will take your savings to double, divide the interest you're earning into 72. If you're earning 8%, divide 8 into 72. Your answer is 9. In nine years, your money will double at 8% interest.

If you have to double what you now have in savings for when you retire in five years, divide 5 into 72. Your answer is 14.4. You must average 14.4% interest over five years to double your money.

By repeating the process, you can calculate quadruples and longer periods of time.

Low interest (fixed, if it goes up) to borrow, unless the rate goes down (variable).

High interest (fixed if rate goes down, variable if it goes up) for earning money.

Little money in checking, more in savings, for interest.

Real estate (buildings, land).

Entrepreneur.

The more money you have, the more money you make. The less money you have, the poorer you get (interest rates being high for borrowing).

Someone once asked Albert Einstein what the most powerful force in the universe was. The brilliant scientist, pausing for effect, quipped, "compound interest".

So Many Savings Choices--Which One is Best?

It seems that *taxable* investments (Roth IRA's, Roth 401k's) are getting a lot of praise lately. They have their place. Try this quick little formula. It can help you know how much you need to earn on taxable investments and savings to equal your *tax-deferred* 401(k)/457 rate.

1. Write in the figure 100.

2. Add up your actual combined federal and state tax percentage.

3. Subtract line two from line one.

Example: 24% federal + 7.5% state = 31.5%. Subtracted from 100 you get 68.5.

4. Write down your annualized rate of return for last year on your 401(k)/457 plan.

5. *Divide* line 3 into line 4. This is the taxable interest rate you must earn to equal your tax-deferred rate.

Example: Say your tax-deferred savings are earning 8%. Divided by 68.5, you get 11.67--your taxable interest rate.

If your taxes are lower, the difference will be less. If you pay higher taxes, the difference is greater.

Can You Actually Retire with More Money Than You Make Now by Working?

Try this simple but amazing financial strategy: 1. You sign on to every wealth maker the system offers, 2. You allow time to become your ally, and 3. You make yourself a more valuable employee.

First, sign on to every wealth maker the system offers. Trust your retirement system to work for you--as it was designed to do.

- This means redepositing any money and interest you may have withdrawn from the system.
- It means religiously putting money into a tax-deferred 401(k) or 457 plan and letting it grow aggressively.
- It means saving through payroll deduction by percent of salary rather than by dollar amount.
- It means using part of every salary raise to increase your 401(k)/457 contributions to your legal or tolerable maximum.

Second, allow time to become your ally. This formula is a get-rich-slow plan. This means you stay with the system throughout your career. *Money Magazine* says, "It appears that staying with one generous employer will produce a higher retirement income than switching among different employers". It means you adhere to your wealth building savings plan, for time is on your side and has a magical way of turning single dollars into hundreds of dollars.

Third, make yourself a more valuable employee. Get additional schooling, a college degree, or advanced degree. Take specialized training and pertinent courses to give yourself more opportunity for salary increases and promotion. Your income will improve while you labor, plus, an improved income creates the lucrative multiplier for both your retirement and Social Security benefits.

Now let's work the formula so you can see what your devotion buys. We'll assume:

- You're married at the time you retire.
- You improved yourself throughout your career.
- You put money into a 401(k) at a planned rate.
- You work 30 years in the system, retiring at age 65.
- Your final average monthly salary is $2,501 (formula works for any salary).

This, then, could be yours:

Source	Monthly
Retirement benefit	$1,303
Social Security benefit(1)	$1,074
Social Security spousal benefit(1)	$ 537
401(k) payout(2)	$ 556
TOTAL MONTHLY BENEFIT	**$3,470**

Final (3 year) Average Salary	Annual Pension Income Retiring at 65
$30,013	$41,640

Can this be true? Cross your heart! If you faithfully follow this strategy, these verifiable figures show what you can realistically expect. Sure, your own salary and service will differ, but the principles are the same. For you it means an instant raise at retirement plus a cost-of-living adjustment of up to 4% on your original retirement benefit after the first year. And don't forget Utah's tax deduction of up to $7,500 per person once you reach age 65.

Since you're getting older whether you play or plan, why not plan to have a pile of money waiting to play with when you arrive?

1. Supplied by the Social Security Administration. Assumes spouse will select the highest paying option. Early

retirement will reduce the benefit permanently.

2. Based on 1.5% employer and $25 personal biweekly contributions at 8% rate of return for 20 years; $8,149 current balance. 20 year payout at current value. Contribution amount, frequency, time, and types and returns of investments will determine accumulation. Delaying withdrawal may increase the installment amount.

(source: *Viewpoint*, Volume 16, Number 2 for members of the Utah Retirement Systems)

Taxes

It's that time of year again when most Americans begin thinking about filing their tax returns. And if you're like most Americans, you're probably dreading that April 15th deadline. So how do you prepare yourself without pulling out your hair?

The first thing you need to do is check your filing status. There are different ways to file depending on your status. Obviously, if you're married you can file a joint return, or you can file separately, which is something you may want to consider if one spouse is earning a lot more--or less-- than the other. If you're single and supporting no one but yourself, you file a single return.

If you're legally separated, divorced, or unmarried and you support someone else--like kids or other relatives--you may be able to qualify for what is called "head of household" status which can give you a more favorable tax treatment than if you file as a single person.

There are certain things you can write off like the usual expenses we all write off every year. But then there are others.

During the first 60 months that you're paying on a student loan, you can deduct the interest payments due on that loan. For 2020, the limit for the amount of interest you can deduct from your taxes is $2,500. However, you can only do this if as a couple, you gross under $140,000 filing jointly or $70,000 for others. If you are married, but choose to file separately from your spouse, you cannot take this deduction at all.

Another write-off you can take is the entire amount of points you paid on your mortgage, if you bought a home last year. If you refinanced for a 30-year mortgage, you can take 1/30 off your taxes.

If you're self-employed, you can write off up to 60 percent of your family health insurance premiums even if they're under the 10 percent limit.

Now, if you are owed a refund, you will want to adjust your exemptions. If you are like 73 million others, you are getting a tax refund this year. That's your first mistake because the average refund is $1,624, which you usually end up blowing on a vacation or something material. The object is to adjust your deductions so that you owe nothing or are owed nothing. Owing, however, is better than being owed.

If you do get a return of about $1,600, that means each month you are paying $133 more than you should be. You are better off putting that money into an investment account or Money Market. If you save that $133 a month and invest it in a good mutual fund, after 40 years at an average rate of 11.2 percent, you will have one million dollars.

If you just take the interest from that $133 a month, which at a 5 to 6 percent return should fall at about $40 at the end of the year, and invest that $40 each year for 40 years at an 11 percent return, after 40 years you would have $23,000. That will provide for a nice vacation. The lesson here is this. If you are getting a refund, raise your exemptions on your W4 form so that less is withheld each pay period.

If you owe, you will want to think about tax credits. There are four major credits that affect large categories of taxpayers. What is great about credits, as opposed to write-offs, is that they reduce your tax dollar for dollar. Write-offs merely reduce your taxable income.

The Earned Income Tax Credit is for working families with children. Couples earning up to $53,330 with two or more kids may qualify for a tax credit of up to $5,920.

The American Opportunity Credit is $2,500 per student during their 4 years of college. So if you have a freshman and sophomore in school at the same time, it could save you $10,000 on your tax bill, but they must be taking at least one half of the normal school load to qualify.

Another credit for families is the Child and Dependent Care Credit. With this credit, you can claim up to 35 percent of your dependent care expenses--payments to a nanny or daycare provider or nurse, for an elderly relative--up to $3,000 per qualifying child.

If you adopt a child, you can receive a credit of up to $14,300. This credit phases out beginning at income of $214,520. It evaporates above $254,520.

Also, there are two major credits for families paying higher education expenses. The American Opportunity Credit, which we have already discussed, and the Lifetime Learning Credit, which is for qualified tuition and related expenses of up to $2,000 per tax return per year. However, you cannot claim both credits for the same student for the same year.

If you haven't yet opened an Individual Retirement Account or you haven't contributed to your already existing fund, it's not too late--you can create and make a contribution to your IRA any time from January 1, up to the filing deadline on April 16.

You can't get an extension for IRA contributions even if you request an extension of time to file the tax return. Your IRA has to be in place and funded before you file your return or by April 16, whichever date is earlier. You may be able to deduct all or a part of your deposit, up to $6,000, depending on your income and filing status. Your tax forms have worksheets that will help you determine whether you can claim a write-off.

Tax preparers tend to be more accurate when they are fresh, as compared to the end of the tax season, so get your taxes done now.

Taxes will always be around, so why not learn about taxes and the credits/deductions that you can take. A credit is a dollar-for-dollar reduction in your taxes; therefore, it is more valuable than a deduction. A deduction is usually subject to percentage limits of your Adjusted Gross Income (AGI).

You take the greater of the Standard Deduction or the Itemized Deduction.

Itemized Deductions:

Charitable contributions--50% of Adjusted Gross Income (AGI)

Mortgage interest.

Child tax credit--up to $2,000 per child under age 17.

Child and dependent care credit--20% to 35% of up to $3,000 of child care and similar costs for a child under age 13, or up to $6,000 for two or more qualifying children. 35% of qualified expenses reduced by one percentage point for each $2,000 (or fraction thereof) of AGI over $15,000 down to 20%.

Miscellaneous deductions--over 2% of AGI: dues, subscriptions to journals, and education that maintains or improves skills, or is required by law or job (CPE--Continuing Professional Education), tax preparation fees, unreimbursed employee expenses.

State and local income taxes.

Real estate taxes.

IRA deduction--$6,000 per individual, phased out if married income is $104,000.

Medical and dental deduction--expenses

$$\text{less: } \underline{10\% \text{ of AGI}}$$

$$\text{deduction}$$

Direct moving expenses are deductible if you move farther than 50 miles, and you are employed there for 39 weeks (basically 9 months) out of the next year.

Of course you need to consult your professional tax preparer on all these tax items because laws and rules change every year.

Flex$ Plan (Cafeteria Plan)

The Flex$ amount may not be changed during the course of the year unless you have a change in your family's status (i.e., marriage, divorce, birth of a child, etc.). Money cannot be transferred between Flex$ accounts, and money that is not claimed, or cannot be claimed, within the plan period guidelines is forfeited. This requires you to plan carefully and estimate your out-of-pocket expenses wisely, so you are not caught off guard by a change in circumstances that does not qualify as a change in family status.

Most of us have health care expenses that health insurance does not cover. In addition, many of us pay a considerable amount of money each year for dependent care expenses. These out-of-pocket expenses take a big bite out of our take home pay. That's why you should get involved in a Flex$ plan that will save you money and help you go farther.

The Flex$ program increases your spendable income by reducing your taxes. It accomplishes this by allowing you to use "before-tax" dollars to pay for specific out-of-pocket health care and dependent care expenses. Employees who do not participate in the Flex$ program will pay the same type of expenses with "after-tax" dollars.

The difference between "before-tax" dollars and "after-tax" dollars is very important. "Before-tax" dollars is your gross pay before Federal, State, and Social Security taxes are calculated and deducted. "After-tax" dollars is the net amount remaining after all taxes have been deducted from your pay. It makes good sense to use "before-tax" dollars to pay for eligible health care and dependent care expenses. However, caution should be used in determining the amount to be deducted from your paycheck for Flex$, as unused funds cannot be returned.

Flex$ Saves Money

Flex$ saves you money because the money contributed to a Flex$ reimbursement account is not taxed. Flex$ deductions are taken out of your gross pay before Federal, State, and Social Security taxes are calculated. This means that your taxable income (the income reflected on your annual W-2 form) is lowered. By lowering your taxable income, you will pay less tax and have more money to spend. Here is an example of how it works. Mary and John both earn $30,000 a year, and pay out of their own pocket $400 for health care and $2,000 for dependent care incurred during the year. Mary decides to enroll in a Flex$ plan. John decides not to participate in a Flex$ plan, but claims the dependent child care credit on his tax return.

	Mary	John
Annual pay	$30,000	$30,000
Before-tax Flex$ contributions (health care and dependent care expenses)		
	-$2,400	$0
Taxable Income	$27,600	$30,000
Federal Tax Credit / Child Care		
	$0	$440
Estimated Income and Social Security Taxes		
	-$5,012	-$5,614
Take-home pay	$22,588	$24,386

After-tax payment of health care and dependent care expenses

$0   -$2,400

Remaining annual spendable income

$22,588 $22,426

Increase in spendable income

$162 $0

    By using the Flex$ reimbursement account, Mary saves $162 in taxes. John, on the other hand, is taxed on his full pay. This means that Mary has $162 more in spendable income, even after paying the same $2,400 in expenses that John paid. Why pay more taxes than you have to? It makes good sense to use a Flex$ reimbursement account to pay for eligible health care and dependent care expenses. Of course, the increase in spendable income will vary depending upon the amount that you decide to set aside in a Flex$ account and your own individual situation.

    Unless your out-of-pocket health care expenses exceed 10% of your total adjusted gross income, you will not be able to claim them on your Federal tax return. For instance, if your adjusted gross income is $20,000, your health care expenses must exceed $1,500--and then only the expenses exceeding $1,500 can be deducted. What can you do about this? Open a Flex$ plan account! Paying out-of-pocket costs with before-tax dollars gives you immediate tax savings and increases your spendable income.

    Take some time to think about the health care needs of your family. Review last year's medical, dental, and vision expenses and those from the year before. Then, estimate your out-of-pocket expenses for the upcoming year considering what your medical and/or dental plans cover and what portion you must pay.

    If you pay for dependent care, estimate the amount you expect to pay over the next year. Consider any changes that will occur in dependent day care costs and in the number of eligible dependents you may claim. Remember to take into account such predictable events as family vacations, children entering school, etc.

A Flex$ reimbursement account should be used for those expenses that you can accurately predict. Ask yourself these questions...

Does anyone in my family wear contacts, glasses, or a hearing aid?

Do my children need orthodontia?

Does my doctor want me to quit smoking?

Do I have any small medical bills, not covered by insurance, that chip away at my hard- earned paycheck?

Do I pay for the care of an incapacitated spouse or dependent parent?

Do I have young children who need day care so I can work?

Do I pay a child care worker to care for my child part of the day?

If you answer yes to any of the above questions, a Flex$ account may be right for you. Why not pay your predictable health care and dependent care expenses with tax-free money?

Retirement

Retirement has frequently been called "The Golden Years", a time during which people will have the time and resources to pursue interests and activities that years of work did not allow. However, many people are poorly prepared for retirement. 78% of all U.S. households will face retirement with less than 50% of the income they'll need after they stop working. The right approach to retirement planning, particularly early in one's life work, can greatly reduce--or even eliminate-- this retirement funding deficit. For many people the key is to participate fully in retirement plans, save more across the board, and consider assuming more investment risk in their portfolio allocations for long-term growth. (Granite Credit Union's "The Counselor", Issue 4, Volume 64)

Financial security in retirement requires regular contributions to a retirement savings plan during your working years.

Investing, 401(k)

When it comes to investing, risk and return are two concepts that go hand in hand, one no more important than the other. None of your investments should be so risky that they cause you to lose sleep. On the other hand, if investors desire a rate of return faster than inflation over the long term, some risk must be assumed. Risk can be viewed as the possibility of your investment losing or not gaining any value.

Minimizing Risk to Maximize Return

One of the best ways to minimize risk while maximizing your return is simply to not put all of your eggs in one basket. In other words, diversify your money by spreading it among several different types of investments. By diversifying your money, you can actually lower your overall risk with the potential of a higher return than if you had all of your money in one investment. The advantage of diversification is that you are not wholly dependent on the performance of a single investment.

Time Horizon is Important

Investors' risk tolerance, as well as the returns they achieve, are greatly impacted by how long they can leave their money invested. If you won't need your money for many years and you are willing to ride out the financial market's ups and downs, you could assume more risk without substantially decreasing your level of comfort. You would then have the potential for higher returns, knowing that time is on your side. In the event of a downturn in the financial markets, you would have time to wait for a market recovery. In the later years, you may consider investing more conservatively because you have less time to ride out any downturns in the market.

A small payment made with regularity produces very profitable results. Nobody can afford not to insure a treasure for retirement and the protection of one's family, even if your business and investments are prosperous.

It is more important how you take care of your money than how much money you actually make. There are many, many people who make a great amount of money but never seem to have enough to provide even the basic necessities of life. But there are also many people who do not make near what these others make yet still manage their resources well enough that they always have plenty. Which will you be?

How Long Will My Money Last?

How much can you withdraw from your savings each month when you retire and have it last as long as you want it to?

If you want your savings to last: multiply the sum available by:

15 years	0.0092701236
20 years	0.0080559319
25 years	0.0073899118

This gives you a monthly income figure from your savings. Example: $10,000 x 0.0080559319 = $80.56 per month over 20 years (assumes 7 1/2% interest and does not calculate the effects of taxes or inflation).

As the stock markets become volatile in moving up and down, you need to remind yourself why you are investing. Were you in it for the short term or long term? If you can't sleep at night and are uncomfortable with your current investments, then it is probably time to change your strategy.

You should invest aggressively when you are young because you will be in it for the long haul. If you are 20 to 30 years away from retirement, you should maintain a balanced portfolio that is heavily weighted in equities. You will probably invest in value and growth funds, with some small cap stocks and foreign funds. You should occasionally rebalance your portfolio, to coincide with market gains and losses, so that an asset does not make up too much of your total investment pie. This strategy will ensure that you do not have "all of your eggs in one basket".

Then, you should move into more conservative investments as you reach retirement. I would suggest allocating 60 percent of your 401(k) to equities and 40 percent to fixed-income holdings, such as money market funds and bond funds, if you hope to retire in about five to seven years.

Insurance

We were first paying $554.90 for auto insurance on two vehicles. Now we pay $462.90. We saved $92.00. You pay more if you pay it in installments. We receive discounts for a good driving record, being over 25 years old, multiple policy, utility car, multiple car, passive restraint, premier plus, and antilock brakes. It would also help to drive less, have a car with a high safety rating, and live in the country instead of the city. It helps to shop around.

We paid $399.00 for house insurance. Now we pay $339.00. We saved $60.00 by shopping around, having our policy with the same carrier as our cars, etc.

Home and Real Estate

Do not get involved with those "FastPay" or "Accelerated Mortgage" plans. All they do is charge you a $10 or $20 fee to process your early mortgage payment. You can just make an extra payment, or increase your payment amount, and have them apply it to principal each time you make your monthly payment. That way you are reducing your mortgage liability without paying extra fees. In short, be smart and keep more of your own money. The plans say that they make it easy for you by automatically making extra principal payments that you may not always remember to do. In essence, the equivalent of one mortgage payment is collected and credited as extra principal each year. Well, you can do that yourself. These programs say that they in no way alter or lessen your existing mortgage contract regarding the amount of the monthly payments, when payments are due, the application of the payments, the assessment of late charges, or the calculation of delinquencies.

When we went to see how much we could qualify for a loan, the mortgage officer did some calculations, and then he said that we would qualify for a $212,000 loan. I thought that was insane and ludicrous because we were both just recent college graduates starting our first "real" jobs. The payment on that kind of loan would have strapped us down like we were in a straight jacket and couldn't move. We wouldn't have been able to do anything else but fret, stress, and have many sleepless nights trying to figure out how to make that payment. Instead, we bought a $130,000 home, lived comfortably, and were happy. Let's buy a home that we can afford and thus ease the payments that will constantly hang over our heads without mercy or respite for as long as thirty years.

On a $150,000 mortgage at 6.625 percent, the monthly principal and interest payment on a 30-year loan would be $960.46. If the interest rate rises to 7.625 percent, the payment rises to $1,061.69--$100 more a month than at the lower rate.

It sure helps to wait for a buyers' market and lock yourself in on a low, fixed interest rate. We waited and got a 6.5% interest rate on a 30-year loan. Then, the market took a downturn and interest rates increased to up over 8%. We saved a bunch of money by patiently waiting, saving, and then getting in at the right time.

It sure helps to save and make a large down payment. Also, if you can put down 20% of the value of your mortgage loan, you don't have to pay exorbitant amounts of money for unnecessary mortgage insurance.

Miscellaneous

We try to gamble our way into prosperity, and, in the process, we further impoverish ourselves. In 1994 alone, Americans spent 482 billion dollars on gambling--more than they spent that year on movies, sports, music, cruise ships, and theme parks combined. Not long ago, lotteries were forbidden by law. Now, in many of our states, they are commonly viewed as a painless and politically expedient way to tax people without really taxing them, and to help balance budgets that are often out of line because of the unrestrained, undisciplined spending of public officials who have squandered their constituents' resources.--Gordon B. Hinckley--"Standing For Something"

The humorous (but often true) golden rule of money says that "He who has the gold makes the rules"--and, we should add, financial opportunities.

Don't gamble because the machines are always fixed against you. You may win once or twice, but the odds are always in favor of the establishment's owner. How else do you think they can continually build multi-million dollar casinos?

I remember going to a casino one time to eat at their buffet. Casinos usually have great buffets for reasonable prices. Buffets, attractions, shows, etc. are persuasive marketing tools to get you inside of the casino, and then while you are there, the casino management assumes you will gamble and spend all of your money. Well anyway, we got there early so we could get a good seat and have plenty of food choices; however, the buffet had not quite opened. Therefore, we stood in line waiting for the doors to open. I noticed that when we first arrived in line, a lady sat down at the slot machines. She had one of those magnetic cards on which they put a certain amount of money, and then you play the machines while fixed sums of money are automatically deducted from your balance. When the lady started gambling, she began with $500 on her card. We stood in line for only fifteen minutes. When the buffet doors opened, this woman had $175 left on her card. In that short period of time, this woman lost $325. I would have hated to have been her.

It takes hard work and determination to get ahead, not just a "quick fix", a "get rich quick scheme", or a "pill" that will solve all of our problems. Don't be misled by these false notions. You do not want to part with your money without first pondering and studying the activity carefully. I got into a small business deal once in which I lost about $100 simply because the environment was not right and the people's needs were not there. That's not to say that the product and service were bad, but maybe I didn't do my homework quite like I should have done. Don't lose your entire principal for "so-called" increased earnings.

If certain warranties do not already come with your purchase of a product, do not buy the warranties, or extended warranties, that the company is pushing. You would be better off just saving money over a period of time, and when something goes wrong and you have an emergency, use your savings to take care of the problem. Many times these warranties only cover you for a short period of time, and they only cover you for specific problems. Often these problems are rare, and the longer time passes, the less the warranties cover.

Companies are becoming very astute in their marketing, advertising, and selling techniques. They are very persuasive and, at times, try to manipulate people. Always read the fine print and know what you are getting into.

We live in an age of persuasive advertising and skillful salesmanship, all designed to entice us to spend--and all too often to spend money we don't have. How can you spend money if you don't even have it in the first place? There would be fewer rash decisions, fewer unwise investments, fewer consequent losses, fewer bankruptcies, if married couples would counsel together on money matters and seek counsel from others. It is a good idea to discuss, consult, and agree on large expenditures.--part by Gordon B. Hinckley

89% of all divorces are caused by money problems.

The fact is that in our current age of fun we spend more of our money and our time trying to satisfy the physical desire for pleasure than ever before in human history. Too many people are living on the very edge of their incomes or beyond. Home equity loans and second mortgages can be had at the snap of one's fingers. Credit cards and other kinds of plastic money are available to nearly everyone over eighteen. Borrowing money is made to appear effortless and desirable, with never a mention of the responsibility to repay. Seductive advertising strives to persuade us that we deserve to have it all and to have it *now*, regardless of the cost. There is a lack of self-discipline and financial self-control that promises future doom.--Gordon B. Hinckley

"Wealth is a power. With wealth many things are possible."-- from The Richest Man in Babylon.

If you by chance "get rich quick", those riches usually flee in much the same way they came. You didn't have to work for it, you therefore don't appreciate it as much, and it will slip from your fingertips easier.

You want to be financially secure and stable so that you can buy things when they are on sale, or there is a good deal. You don't want to be in a bind and have to buy the item at full price when you also may not have any money.

We are moving into the most competitive world this world has ever seen. All around us is competition. We need all the education we can get. The world will in large measure pay us what it thinks we are worth, and our worth will increase as we gain education and proficiency in our chosen field.

The 5-Finger System to Financial Freedom

Ask yourself, "Am I financially happy, or am I financially unhappy?"

Many people try to find happiness and fulfillment in activities that are illegal, immoral, or unethical. Others seek only to have fun in life. With this as their main goal. they allow *temporary* pleasure to distract them from *lasting* happiness. There can be problems with society, the stock market, global economies, subprime mortgages, jumbo loans, lending problems, quick-cash shops that charge you very high interest rates, etc.

Here is a 5-Finger System to Financial Freedom:

1. Pay Tithing and Offerings

Financial freedom begins with the payment of tithing and being generous in your charitable offerings. The Lord says in the bible that he will open the windows of heaven and pour you out great blessings that there will not be room enough to receive them when you faithfully pay your tithes and offerings. And he will rebuke the devourer for your sakes. Faithful tithe payers learn that they cannot afford *not* to pay tithing. In a very literal and wonderful way, the windows of heaven are opened and blessings are poured out upon them.

2. Avoid Debt

Discipline yourself in your purchases to avoid debt. Avoid debt, with the exception of buying a modest home and paying for a quality education. If you are in debt, pay it off as quickly as possible. Free yourself from this bondage. Save money to purchase what you need. There is an adage, "use it up, wear it out, make it do, or do without." Benjamin Franklin said, "The borrower is a slave to the lender, and the debtor to the creditor, disdain the chain, preserve your freedom; and maintain your independency. Be industrious and free; be frugal and free." Remember Wimpy in Popeye the Sailor Man who said, "I will gladly pay you Tuesday for a hamburger today." You do *not* want to be like Wimpy!

3. Use a Budget

Keep a record of your inflows and outflows. Review monthly your income and expenses. Determine how to reduce what you spend for any non-essential items. You might have to sell some things, change spending habits, or maybe move into a more affordable home. Use this information to establish a budget. Plan what your income is, how much you will save, and determine what you spend for food, housing, utilities, transportation, clothing, insurance, etc. Don't sacrifice what you *really* want tomorrow for what you *think* you want today. It's kind of like going shopping at the grocery store when you are hungry. It all looks so good and you want it now because you are starving to death. But, after you get home and eat, you have buyer's regret thinking that some of that food is not good for you, you bought too much, and it is too expensive as well. There is a difference between For Sale and On Sale. Shrink your expenses to fit your income. Don't spend that which you do not have. Review your budget regularly. Discipline yourself to live within your budget. Or in other words, live within your means. If your outflows exceed your inflows, your upkeep will be your downfall. Remember one tough rule of life and finances: *You can't have everything*. Also, you can't have everything now, which may have taken your parents, or some people, 20, 30, or even 40 years to acquire or accumulate. Spending less money than you make is essential to your financial security and well-being.

4. Save for a Rainy Day

Gradually build up a financial reserve, and then you will have it to use for emergencies such as unemployment or sickness. Storms seem to come, and it's good to have money set aside for a rainy day. Regularly save a little money and it will accumulate into a great sum over time.

5. Teach Your Family

Teach your family members these prior four principles of financial management. Involve your family in creating a budget and setting family financial goals. Teach them principles of hard work, frugality, and saving. Be deliberate about the money decisions you make. We are not limited by them, but rather empowered by them. When you work together, you will enjoy greater peace in your hearts and you will achieve financial freedom.

Real Estate Investing

Tax Benefits for Real Estate Investors

- Depreciation - Every year for 27.5 years you get a deduction just for owning real estate.
- More Depreciation - Not only can you depreciate the buildings, you can also depreciate the parts that make them inhabitable, such as HVAC, water heaters, plumbing, and light fixtures.
- Taxes/Insurance/Utilities - You can deduct all of the real estate taxes, insurance, and utility charges you have already paid.
- Repairs - Repairs and supplies needed for upkeep ate deductible.
- Fees - Fees to accountants to do your taxes are also deductible.
- Home Office - If you work from home, you can take the home office deduction. This means you can deduct a portion of your home's expenses, such as: mortgage payments, tax and insurance, utility payments, etc.
- Office Deduction - Office supplies and equipment are deductible. If you use it to run your real estate business, chances are it's deductible.
- Business Expenses - You probably use the internet to search for real estate listings and information. You probably paid membership fees to become part of a real estate association. You might be a Realtor and pay for

annual licensing. You probably go to seminars to learn new real estate techniques. All are likely deductible.
- **Mileage** Keep a log of the miles driven related to your real estate business.
- **Qualified Real Estate Professional** - If you are a qualified real estate professional, there really is no limit to the deductions. Go full time to take full advantage of this.

Be sure to check with your CPA to ensure that you are taking full advantage of the tax deductions available to you.

The Tri-Fecta of real estate investing is 1) cash flow, 2) depreciation, and 3) appreciation.

Retirement

The number of years of experience in real estate determines who you are and what you do:

0 - 10 years -- you are a Starter

11 - 30 years -- you are a Builder

31 - 40 years -- you are a Finisher

Questions you should ask yourself that relate to retirement are:

> At what age do you want to retire?
>
> How much gross Annual Income do you want at retirement?
>
> What Cap Rate is your target?
>
> At retirement, what percentage do you want to own free and clear vs. have debt on?
>
> Therefore, how much in total real estate assets do you need to retire?

    If you have a good plan and it works out well over your working life, then you can maybe retire at age 55 or 60. If the economy had some bumps in the road and things don't go as well according to your plan, you may have to retire a little later at age 65 or 67.

    The cap rate, or capitalization rate, is equal to the net operating income (NOI) divided by the purchase price of the property. In certain areas or maybe for multi-family, the cap rate might be 3% to 4%. In other areas, the cap rate might be 4% to 6%. The average cap rate might be 5%, which is good. If you can get a cap rate of 8% to 10%, then that would be great.

So, to use the information above, you may want to have $100,000 a year in annual income, you might have a target cap rate of 5%, and you want to own your properties free and clear and not have any debt on them. Therefore, using the calculation of Annual Income ($100,000)/Cap Rate (5%)/Debt Coverage (100%), you will need $2,000,000 in total real estate assets when you retire.

Multiple Streams of Income

1. Working
2. Spouse Working
3. Pension
4. Spouse Pension
5. Social Security
6. Spouse Social Security
7. Real Estate Business (Cash Flow, Depreciation, Appreciation)
8. Accounting Business
9. Interest (Investments, Stocks, Bonds, Mutual Funds, Money Market, Savings, 401k, IRA, HSA, 529 Plan)
10. Dividends
11. Asset Appreciation
12. Insurance Proceeds - Indexed Annuity
13. Gifts
14. Internet Business
15. Book Royalty Income

Your income streams should be connected. You need to have symbiotic flows. For example, in real estate, you can be the developer, the contractor, the owner, have laundry facilities in the complex, etc.

You can pick up a second job, do a side job, generate passive income, etc.

3 Tips to Becoming Wealthy

To some extent, it's how much money you make. But, it's also about having your money work for you and how much of that money you actually can keep.

Even if you earn a modest salary, you can use these 3 tips to become a millionaire:

Start Early

When you're young, time is on your side. The sooner you start putting your money to work, the less you'll have to save each month to reach your goals. This is the beauty of compound interest. It's a powerful principle.

[If you start at age 23, for instance, you only have to save about $14 a day to be a millionaire by age 67. That's assuming a six percent average annual investment return.

If you start at age 35, on the other hand, you'd have to set aside $30 a day to reach seven figure status by age 67.

You can even build a multimillion-dollar portfolio on a modest salary if you start young. Check out how much you have to save per paycheck to have $2 million stashed away by the time you're 67.] -- someone else's words

Invest Every Single Day

Make daily deposits into an investment account. Start small, like maybe $5 or $10, and then you can build up to more and more over time. Set a minimum daily deposit amount. Then eventually try to set aside $100 a day. The important part is that you stick with it. Don't miss a day.

Automate Your Finances

Once you are committed to investing your money, an essential habit to build wealth over time is to automate your finances. The easiest way to do this is to have money from your paycheck or checking account sent directly to your investment account every month before you can even see it. This tip works great because it becomes out of sight and out of mind. It saves you time and you don't even have to worry about it. But, it is so powerful because you can become a millionaire.

Cut out the morning run to the convenience store to grab a coffee, a drink, a burrito, or other breakfast food items. I see so many people stopping off in the morning at convenience stores around my home and where I work. I've already had an inexpensive, but filling, breakfast of pancakes, sausage, and milk that's made with love at home, while many of these other people I see are in the rat race of fighting for a parking space at the convenience store to spend their $5 on breakfast.

Eliminate the $15 lunches that you eat out every day. I have had co-workers and employees for years that go out to lunch every single day of the year. I bring a healthy and filling lunch to work, and it might cost me $5 for lunch each day. That's a savings of $2,500 a year. This also saves me the time of going out to a restaurant every day, and I am more productive with the time I spend at work.

Conclusion

In the Bible, we hear of the parable of the talents. The servant that was given five talents gained another five talents. The servant that was given two talents gained another two talents. But, the servant that was given one talent was fearful of losing that talent, and he went and buried it. Later, the Lord came and took away that one talent and gave it unto him that had ten talents.

It matters very little how much we are given to begin with, for as the parable says, we are given according to our abilities--and some have more abilities than others. However, as long as we are earnestly striving to add upon what has been entrusted to us, God will bless us, and give us more to be stewards over. But, if we are slothful, and don't seek to increase our talents while here in this life, the talents we do have will be taken from us and given to those who have many.

We fool ourselves when we believe we have possessions in this life, but in truth we have nothing but what has been given us by God. We came into this world with nothing, and that is the way we leave it. During the time of our mortal lives we are merely stewards over that which we have. The important thing is that we be wise stewards, seeking to honestly increase what has been given. We can't have more unless we can take care of what we already have.

Paul wrote in one of his letters to Timothy: "For we brought nothing into this world, and it is certain we can carry nothing out. And having food and raiment let us be therewith content. But they that will be rich fall into temptation and a snare, and into many foolish and hurtful lusts, which drown men in destruction and perdition. For the love of money is the root of all evil: which while some coveted after, they have erred from the faith, and pierced themselves through with many sorrows" (1 Timothy 6:7-10).

Now, money itself is not evil. It is the relentless pursuit of wealth at the expense of everything else--including personal integrity and valor--that too often leads to debauchery.--Gordon B. Hinckley

We need to make it a habit to be financially stable and successful.

"We first make our habits, then our habits make us." Anonymous

First we form our habits, then they form us. Conquer your bad habits or they'll conquer you.--Dr. Rob Gilbert

Money....

It can buy you a House
But not a Home

It can buy you a Bed
But not Sleep

It can buy you a Clock
But not Time

It can buy you a Book
But not Knowledge

It can buy you a Position
But not Respect

It can buy you Medicine
But not Health

It can buy you Blood
But not Life

So you see, money isn't everything. The best things in life can't be bought, and often we destroy ourselves trying! anonymous

I confess that I was once like the young man who equated security with money and money with success. I was able to help him see where his perspective was off because life had taught me that true contentment and total success came from the things money can't buy. Don't misunderstand. I like the things money can buy, and I'll bet you do too. I like nice clothes, a beautiful residence, big, comfortable cars, and so on. However, I love the things money won't buy. It will buy me a house, but not a home; a bed, but not a good night's sleep; pleasure, but not happiness; and a good time, but not peace of mind. Success is not equal to money. True success involves every area of your life.--Zig Ziglar's Little Instruction Book, page 111.

Many people honestly believe they will be happy when they get into a home of their own; they will be happy when they get all of the little things that frequently convert a house into a home-- but they won't. Then they'll be happy when they get the mortgage paid--but they won't. Then they will be happy when they get their second home down at the lake or up on the mountainside--but they won't.

The reason is simple: It makes no difference where you go, there you are. And it makes no difference what you have, there's always more to want. Until you are happy with who you are, you will never be happy because of what you have.

The possession of wealth alone does not produce happiness.

Our affections are often too highly placed upon paltry, perishable objects. The things of this world make little or no difference in the happiness of an individual. --Brigham Young

Men for the sake of getting a living forget to live.--Quentin Crisp

We live the life we choose--we are all, right now, living the life of our own choosing. The choices we are talking about are made daily, hourly, moment by moment.--anonymous

We make a living by what we get. We make a life by what we give.--Winston Churchill

Pleasure is short and temporary. Pleasure is spending money, buying items, acquiring toys, going on trips and vacations, etc. These items are all external. However, joy is long-lasting, permanent, and eternal. Joy is having self-worth, family, having a good attitude, being grateful, humble, and being happy, etc. These items are all internal. There really is a difference between joy and pleasure. You will never be able to invest in yourself and have wealth if you are always living for pleasure instead of living to have joy and be happy.

You must choose, but choose wisely.

Investing in yourself is the best investment you can make.

As you apply the principles in this book, you will grow your Money: to the Power of 10!

About the Author

Gayland R Jones is a Certified Public Accountant. Mr. Jones graduated from Southern Utah University with a Masters of Accountancy degree. He also completed his Bachelor of Arts Composite Major in Accounting and Business Administration from that same institution, as well as earning a Spanish Minor. Mr. Jones presently is the CFO/Controller of Double ROC Properties and the Granite Education Foundation in Salt Lake City, Utah. Mr. Jones enjoys sports, hunting, fishing, and the outdoors. Mr. Jones served a two-year church mission in Argentina. He is married to Kammie Bradshaw Jones. They are the parents of three children, and they reside in Taylorsville, Utah.

www.ingramcontent.com/pod-product-compliance
Lightning Source LLC
Chambersburg PA
CBHW070808220526
45466CB00002B/597